WHAT IS A HABITAT?

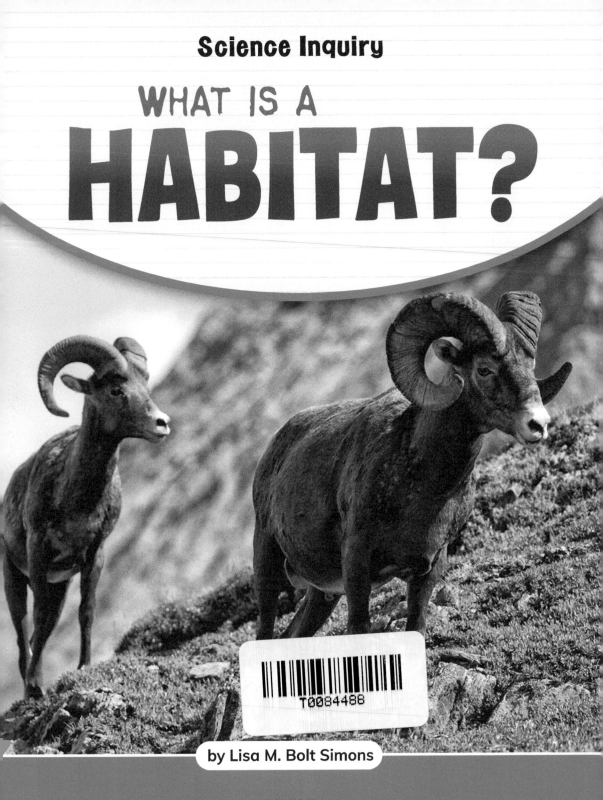

T0084488

by Lisa M. Bolt Simons

PEBBLE
a capstone imprint

Pebble Explore is published by Pebble, an imprint of Capstone.
1710 Roe Crest Drive
North Mankato, Minnesota 56003
www.capstonepub.com

Library of Congress Cataloging-in-Publication Data
Names: Simons, Lisa M. B., 1969- author.
Title: What is a habitat? / Lisa M. Bolt Simons.
Description: North Mankato, Minnesota : Pebble, [2022] | Series: Science inquiry | Includes bibliographical references and index. | Audience: Ages 5-8 | Audience: Grades 2-3 | Summary: "Some animals live in water. Some animals live on land. The land that animals live on can be very different. What makes a place the right home for an animal? Let's investigate habitats!"— Provided by publisher.
Identifiers: LCCN 2021002743 (print) | LCCN 2021002744 (ebook) | ISBN 9781977131454 (hardcover) | ISBN 9781977132628 (paperback) | ISBN 9781977155306 (pdf) | ISBN 9781977156921 (kindle edition)
Subjects: LCSH: Habitat (Ecology)—Juvenile literature.
Classification: LCC QH541.14 .S555 2022 (print) | LCC QH541.14 (ebook) | DDC 577—dc23
LC record available at https://lccn.loc.gov/2021002743
LC ebook record available at https://lccn.loc.gov/2021002744

Image Credits
Getty Images/Dobrila Vignjevic, 29; Shutterstock: acceptphoto, 16, Andii111, 9, Andrea Izzotti, 1, 7 (top right), Anton Petrus, 6 (tr), BGSmith, 15, Big on Wild-Wildlife, 14, Bildagentur Zoonar GmbH, 7 (bottom left), Bruce MacQueen, 13, Choksawatdikorn, 22, COULANGES, 20, David Rasmus, 28, dba duplessis, 25, Enrico Pescantini, 26, GUDKOV ANDREY, 18, HelloRF Zcool, 6 (bottom right), IamJamesAnthony, 7 (top left), isabel kendzior, 11, JaySi, 6 (bl), Jim Cumming, 19, Justin M Croteau, 21, lisnic, cover, Ljupco Smokovski, 5, papkin, 24, Petr Salinger, 12, r.classen, 6 (tl), Rich Carey, 23, StoneMonkeyswk, 7 (br), Susan Flashman, 27, SZakharov, 17

Artistic elements: Shutterstock/balabolka

Editorial Credits
Editor: Erika L. Shores; Designers: Dina Her and Juliette Peters; Media Researcher: Kelly Garvin; Production Specialist: Tori Abraham

TABLE OF CONTENTS

Words in **bold** are in the glossary.

YOUR HABITAT

Do you ever think about what you need to survive? Your favorite game? Your favorite book? Does a game or book help you live? No, you need food to live! Food is part of a **habitat**. A habitat is the place where an animal lives, eats, grows, and stays safe.

What does a person need to stay safe? A table, chair, tablet, or an apartment? An apartment is a place to stay safe. A family has food and water here. An apartment is a habitat!

A HABITAT INVESTIGATION

Let's investigate which habitats are best for animals. Look at the photos of four habitats and four animals. Where might each animal best survive?

mountain   **desert**

savanna   **wetland**

Think about the food animals will find. Think about where they'll find water. Where will the animal find a safe place to sleep and stay away from **predators**? Make a list of which animals belong in each habitat for your investigation.

elephant   **bighorn sheep**

lizard   **heron**

People eat fruit and vegetables. Some people like to eat meat. Food and water are needed to live. Most people sleep on a bed. What's more important is that they have a home, or **shelter**, to keep them warm and safe.

It's the same with animals. They need shelter to keep them safe from predators. They also need shelter to raise **offspring**. Habitats also provide animals with food and water. Habitats are important for a **species** to survive.

WHERE ARE HABITATS?

Habitats are found all over the world. Their locations make them unique. The food and shelter will look different in different places. Habitats differ because of their **climates** too. This is how the weather is over time in a place.

Habitats at the polar ends of Earth are cold. In winter the day is like night. It's dark. The land is always icy and frozen.

A rain forest has a totally different climate than a polar habitat. Rain forests are near the **equator**. Because of this, rain forests get lots of sunshine and heat. They also get plenty of rain.

A woodland is another kind of forest. This habitat has all four seasons. The tall trees have large leaves. Deer and groundhogs are some of the animals in this habitat.

Now let's turn to open spaces. Grasslands are the opposite of forests. They have few or no trees. Wild grasses grow here.

There are two types of grasslands. Tropical **savannas** are warm all year. Think where elephants stroll and lions prowl in Africa.

Temperate savannas are warm in summer but cold in winter. These places are often called prairies. Prairie dogs, mice, and foxes live here.

A desert is a habitat where little rain falls. Some deserts are hot. The Sahara in Africa is hot. Snakes like cobras live here.

A cool desert is the Gobi Desert in Asia. Wild camels and small animals called marmots live here.

A desert can also be freezing! Most of Antarctica is a polar desert. Very little rain or snow falls. Penguins are made to live in this habitat.

A mountain is a habitat where the ground rises to a **summit**. As the **elevation** goes up, the climate gets cooler. Snow never melts on the tops of some mountains.

Forests can grow on the lower parts of mountains. Mountain gorillas live in these forests in Africa.

Some animals can live high above mountain forests. Snow leopards live up to 18,000 feet (5,486 meters) high in the mountains of Asia.

Water covers much of Earth. That means many habitats are **aquatic**, or in water.

Freshwater habitats don't have a lot of salt. Rivers are flowing bodies of water. River dolphins live in these habitats in South America and Asia.

Other freshwater habitats are ponds, lakes, and wetlands. Loons and many other kinds of birds live in wetland habitats.

Marine habitats have salt in the water. Oceans cover about 75 percent of Earth. That's a huge habitat full of animals! Oceans are home to huge blue whales. Zooplankton live in oceans too. Some are so tiny, you need a microscope to see them.

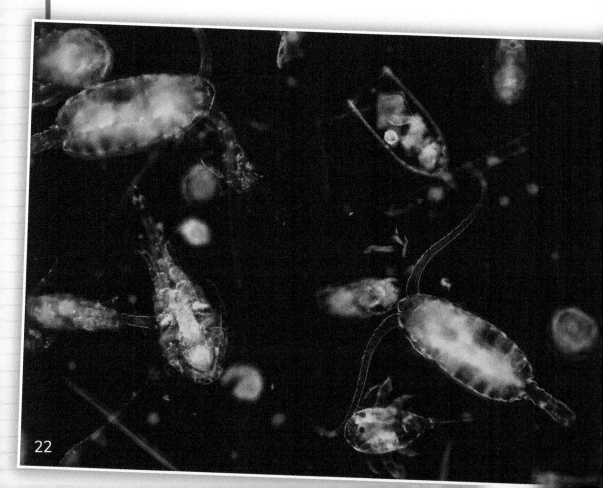

Coral reefs are habitats found only in warm ocean water. Sea snakes and starfish are just a few of the animals living here.

WHAT KINDS OF HOMES ARE IN HABITATS?

No matter the habitat, animals need shelter. They need to keep themselves safe from predators and the weather.

Shelter comes in different forms. Think about people. They live in houses, apartments, trailer homes, tents, or huts.

Some animals build their homes. Spiders weave webs. Moles dig holes under the ground.

Other animals use shelters that they find. Bats live in caves. A porcupine's den is inside a tree trunk.

WHY ARE THERE ANIMAL ADAPTATIONS IN HABITATS?

But an animal just can't live where there's shelter. A walrus doesn't have the **adaptations** to live in the desert. Its body is for the water. Its blubber keeps it warm. A sloth won't make it in a coral reef. Its sharp claws are for climbing trees.

Animals also can't live wherever there is food. Koalas only eat leaves of eucalyptus trees. Their bodies are adapted to these leaves. Koalas wouldn't survive in a beaver's habitat. They couldn't eat bark!

Remember what you need to stay alive. You don't need your favorite game or book. You need food, water, and shelter.

It's the same with animals. They only live in habitats that fit these needs. Animals have adaptations that work in their habitats.

You can help wild animals and their habitats. Pick up trash. Help clean up parks and other nature areas. Plant flowers and trees. Keep habitats safe and healthy for the animals that live there.

GLOSSARY

adaptation (a-dap-TAY-shuhn)—a change a living thing goes through in order to fit, or survive in its surroundings

aquatic (uh-KWAH-tik)—growing or living in water all or most of the time

climate (KLY-muht)—the usual weather in a place

elevation (e-luh-VAY-shuhn)—the height to which something can reach

equator (i-KWAY-tuhr)—an imaginary line around the middle of Earth

habitat (HAB-uh-tat)—the natural home of an animal or plant

offspring (OF-spring)—the young of an animal

predator (PRED-uh-tur)—an animal that hunts other animals for food

savanna (suh-VAN-uh)—a flat, grassy area with few or no trees

shelter (SHEL-tur)—a place where an animal can stay safe from weather and other animals

species (SPEE-sheez)—a group of animals or plants with common characteristics or features

summit (SUHM-it)—the very top of a mountain

temperate (tem-PUR-ayt)—not too hot, cold, or wet

READ MORE

Murray, Julie. *Animals in Antarctica*. Minneapolis: Abdo Publishing, 2020.

Newland, Sonya. *Habitats*. North Mankato, MN: Capstone Press, 2020.

Topacio, Francine. *Creatures in a Wet Rain Forest*. New York: PowerKids Press, 2020.

INTERNET SITES

Habitats
kids.nationalgeographic.com/explore/nature/habitats/

Habitats: Habitat Basics
pbs.org/video/habitat-habitat-basics-buxg6x/

World Biomes: Coral Reefs
kids.nceas.ucsb.edu/biomes/coralreef.html

INDEX